CRYPTOCURRENCY DEFINED

CRYPTOCURRENCY
DEFINED

YOUR GUIDE TO CRYPTOCURRENCY AND THE FUTURE OF THE INTERNET

PHOENIX MARCÓN, CHC, CLC
AUSTIN AKERS

MARCÓN
—PRESS—

Printed by: Marcón Press
Cover Design by Marcón Marcón Press
Layout Design: Marcón Press
Prepared for Printing by Karthik Parameswaran

Author Contact: P.O. Box 737 | Allen, TX 75002
                  PhoenixMarcon.com

Library Congress Cataloging-in-Publication Data
Marcón, Phoenix
          Cryptocurrency Defined/Phoenix Marcón. p. cm.
          1. Cryptocurrency   2. Investing   3. Finance

Paperback - ISBN 978– 0-9895934-0-3

10 9 8 7 6 5 4 3 2 1

FOLLOW ME ON SOCIAL MEDIA

First Edition

OTHER BOOKS BY PHOENIX MARCÓN

FICTION: CARNATION

SELF-HELP: LUMINARIES, vol. I

                            JOURNAL—Reflections

                            Pocket of Inspiration

HEALTH: START HERE - Ketogenics for Beginners

POETRY: Thoughts of Wonder

BUSINESS: Better Business Book (co-authored)

                            Hustle Code

                            Entrepreneurial Hustle

                            BLOCKCHAIN Defined

(Coming Soon)

CULINARY: Date Night

FICTION: Beautiful People (Saga)

NON-FICTION: LUMINARIES, vol. II

                            LUMINARIES, vol. III

HUMOR: Jocose

More to come…

DISCLAIMER

This book is presented solely for educational and entertainment purposes. The author and publisher are not offering it as legal, financial, accounting, or other professional services advice. While best efforts have been used in preparing this book, the author and publisher make no representations or warranties of any kind and assume no liabilities of any kind with respect to the accuracy or completeness of the contents and specifically disclaim any implied warranties of merchantability of use for a particular purpose. Neither the author nor the publisher shall be held liable or responsible to any person or entity with respect to any loss or incidental or consequential damages caused, or alleged to have been caused, directly or indirectly, by the information or programs contained herein. Every individual is different and the advice and strategies contained herein may not be suitable for your situation. You should seek the services of a competent professional before beginning any improvement program. The story and its characters and entities are fictional. Any likeness to actual persons, either living or dead, is strictly coincidental.

"Virtual currencies, perhaps most notably Bitcoin, have captured the imagination of some, struck fear among others, and confused the heck out of the rest of us."

– Thomas Carper, US-Senator

TABLE OF CONTENTS

1

WHAT IS CRYPTOCURRENCY?

What is cryptocurrency? I'm sure many of you are curious about this so-called "21st-century money of the future, and due to its increasing recognition and security, the cryptocurrency market looks bright ahead.

By the end of this book, you'll undoubtedly know more about cryptocurrency than most people out there. For this first chapter, we will be covering five topics:

- What Is Cryptocurrency?
- How Do Cryptocurrencies Work?
- How Are the Cryptocurrencies Value Determined?
- What Is Cryptocurrency Used For?
- Why Cryptocurrency?

What Is Cryptocurrency?

This is one of the most frequently asked questions out there. What is cryptocurrency? Cryptocurrency is derived from the word "Cryptography," which refers to the consensus-keeping process secured by strong cryptography. To make it simple, cryptocurrency is a digital version of money where the transactions are done online. A cryptocurrency is a medium of exchange just like your normal currency such as the USD but designed to securely exchange digital information through a process known as cryptography.

The first ever-successful cryptocurrency emerged from the invention of Bitcoin, by Satoshi Nakamoto. This was then followed by the birth of other types of cryptocurrencies such as Ethereum, Ripple, Litecoin and more competing against Bitcoin.

How Do Cryptocurrencies Work?

The reason why cryptocurrencies are in such demand right now is that Satoshi Nakamoto successfully found a way to build a decentralized digital cash system. What is a decentralized cash system?

A decentralized system means its users power the network without having any third party, central authority or middleman controlling it. Not the central bank or the government has power over this system.

The problem with a centralized network in a payment system is the so-called "double spending." Double spending happens when one entity spends the same amount twice. For instance, when you purchase things online, you have to incur for unnecessary and expensive transaction fees. Usually, this is done by a central server that keeps track of your balances.

This is most commonly known as the Blockchain Technology.

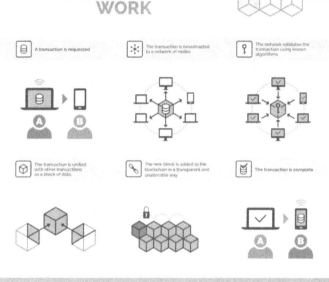

Blockchain technology functions in managing and maintaining a growing set of data blocks and this are done by using the decentralized P2P (Peer to Peer) network. In blockchain, once a piece of data is recorded, it cannot be edited or changed, only updated on a new block.

To put it in simpler terms, it enables you to send a gold coin via email. The P2P network is a consensus network, which allows a new payment system and the transactions of new digital money.

Let's illustrate an example. Cryptocurrency like Bitcoin consists of its network of peers. Every peer has a record of the complete history of all transactions as well as the balance of every account.

By the end of every transaction and upon confirmation, the transaction is known almost immediately by the whole network. A transaction includes a process where A gives X number of Bitcoins to B and is signed by A's private key. After signed, a transaction is broadcasted in the network. The information is sent from one peer to every other peer on the web.

Confirmation is a critical stage in the cryptocurrency system. Evidence is everything. When the transaction is not confirmed it's thrown out, unless 51% or more can agree it's valid.

When a transaction is confirmed, it is set in stone. It can't be reversed; it is impossible to be hacked, it is not forgeable as it is part of a permanent record of the historical transaction: The Blockchain.

The blockchain can be likened to an online ledger, where all transactions are recorded and made visible to the whole network.

This comes to show that cryptocurrencies are not secured by people or trust, but by complex mathematical equations. It is very secure, and it's highly unlikely that the address of a currency is compromised.

Only miners can confirm a transaction. This is their role in the cryptocurrency network. They record transactions, verify them and disperse the transactional information in the network.

For every completed transaction monitored and facilitated by the miners, they are rewarded with a token of cryptocurrency, for instance with Bitcoins.

Since miners play a significant role in the cryptocurrency system, let's look at their position in more detail.

What Are Miners Doing?

First and foremost, principally anyone can be a miner. Miners are needed because of the nature of the decentralized network where they have no authority to delegate tasks, and the cryptocurrency needs some kind of system

To prevent any form of network abuse. For instance, a person may create thousands of peers and spread forged transactions. It will disrupt the system immediately.

In order for you to be a miner, you would need to solve a cryptologic puzzle which is a set of very complex mathematical questions known as a hash; this structure was set by Satoshi Nakamoto himself. If you successfully solved the problem, as a miner, you can build a block and add it to the blockchain.

In simple terms, hashing means taking an input string of any length and giving out an output of a fixed length. In the context of cryptocurrencies like Bitcoin, the transactions are taken as an input and run through a hashing algorithm which gives an output of a fixed length.

The miner is also given permission to add a cryptocurrency transaction to the system which automatically grants him a specific number of bitcoins. This is the only way to create valid bitcoins. Bitcoins can only be generated if a miner can  solve a cryptographic puzzle. The level of difficulty increases and more currency is introduced into the eco-system.

How Are the Cryptocurrencies Value Determined?

The value of cryptocurrencies is dependent on the market, where the prices of various cryptocurrencies vary a lot and are one of the most fluctuating and volatile markets to date.

The price of cryptocurrencies like any other products is dependent on demand and supply. If more people demand a particular currency and it is short in supply, then the value increases. More units are mined by miners to balance the flow. However, most coins limit the number of their tokens. It's like gold, there is a limited supply.

For instance, the total amount of Bitcoin issued is only 21 million.

Therefore, Bitcoin's supply will decrease in time and will reach its final number by 2140. It also explains why Bitcoin's value is higher as compared to other cryptocurrencies.

Now you must be wondering, what is cryptocurrency used for?

Cryptocurrencies can be spent for different purposes, and the best part is, all transactions are completed online! There are three separate transactions that can be performed when using cryptocurrency:

- Trading
- Personal Spending
- Crowdfunding

Firstly, is **Trading.**

Trading can be very profitable for both professionals and beginners. The market is new, where arbitrage and margin trading are widely available. The currency's high volatility has also played a major role in bringing new investors to the trading market.

Compared to other financial currencies, cryptocurrency has minimal barrier to entry. If you already own cryptocurrency, no verification is required, and you can start trading almost instantly. Moreover, cryptocurrency is not a fiat currency. This just means the price is not related to the economy or policies of any single country.

And unlike stock markets, there are no official exchanges. Instead, hundreds of exchanges   operate 24/7 around the world. Because of no formal exchanges, this results in no official price where the currency is known for its rapid and frequent price movements.

Secondly is **Personal Spending.**
You can use cryptocurrency to purchase almost anything! From buying cars to traveling the world.

In December 2013, a Tesla Model S was purchased for a reported 91.4 Bitcoins. The dealer, located in California continues to accept Bitcoin as a means of payment. They have since managed to sell a Lamborghini Gallardo for 216.8 Bitcoin.

You can also travel the world using Bitcoins! Just head to www.cheapair.com. On 22nd November 2013, they announced that they would be the first online traveling agency accepting Bitcoin. You can purchase flights, hotels, car rentals and cruises. You can even book the whole package.

Cryptocurrency also provides the chance for you to give back to society. How? By **Crowdfunding.** You can be part of someone's success story by donating to a crypto crowdfunding project. Companies such as Lighthouse have built their crowdfunding platform using Bitcoin.

The perks of donating through this system are you will not be charged for your donation and funds will not be released unless the project meets its criteria. You are also able to withdraw from the campaign before its completion.

You have complete control over the donation! Examples of successful funding campaigns are from Dogecoin, which includes campaign runs for NASCAR driver Josh Wise.

The question is, Why Cryptocurrency?

Apart from cryptocurrency being very secure and is run through a decentralized network, there are other properties which project why cryptocurrencies may be the most talked about topic in town. It has also been considered as potentially an investment vehicle, which may garner large returns.

Have you heard of Erik Finman? The teenage Bitcoin millionaire who started picking up Bitcoin at only $12 a piece back in May 2011, when he was just 12 years old. He received the Bitcoin as a tip from his brother and a $1000 gift from his grandmother.

He now reportedly owns 403 Bitcoins, which holds a value of roughly $2,600 where it has accumulated to a stash of $1.08 million and change.

There are various concrete reasons why you should invest in cryptocurrency. This will be elaborated further in chapter 6, but let me give you a summary of the perks of buying cryptocurrency.

Firstly, are its transactional properties. Cryptocurrency transactions are fast and global compared to traditional banking. Transactions are propagated immediately in the network and are confirmed within minutes. Since a worldwide network of computers manages the trades, they do not take into account your physical location. It is possible for you to send your cryptocurrency to someone in your vicinity, or even if they are living on the other side of the world with ease.

Secondly, are its store of value properties. The currencies are in controlled supply; thus there is a high chance that the value of the currencies appreciates over time. As mentioned earlier, Bitcoin will somehow reach its final number somewhere in 2140.

The third is its revolutionary property. You have more control over what is going on in your account and how the system works and operate. This is due to the decentralized network of peers which keeps a consensus on account balances and the transactions made. As compared to your physical bank account, which can be changed and controlled by people you don't see and governed by rules you don't even know?

2

TYPES OF CRYPTOCURRENCY

The world of cryptocurrency has always revolved around Bitcoin until recently when virtual currencies have served a significant purpose in the investment realm, and people start flocking to cryptocurrencies as compared to fiat currencies.

Believe it or not, aside from Bitcoin, there are over 2000

cryptocurrencies according to coin market cap. However, we will only discuss the top 5 most prominent currencies in the market. The five cryptocurrencies are:

- *Bitcoin (BTC)*
- *Ethereum (ETH)*
- *Litecoin (LTC)*
- *Monero (XMR)*
- *Ripple (XRP)*

Firstly, is **Bitcoin.**

This is the first ever cryptocurrency invented and remains by far the most sought-after cryptocurrency to date. Bitcoin is known as the digital gold standard in the cryptocurrency network. As explained in the previous module, Bitcoin is the pioneer of Blockchain Technology that made digital money possible.

It is the first ever decentralized peer-to-peer network powered by its users without any central authority or middleman which means, no unnecessary costs are included in the digital money transaction.

Over the years of Bitcoin's existence, its value has fluctuated tremendously from zero to over $19000 per Bitcoin to date. Its transaction volume has also reached 200,000 daily transactions.

One significant advantage that it has over other cryptocurrencies is bitcoins are impossible to counterfeit or inflate. The reason being there are only 21 million bitcoins created for mining, no more no less. Therefore, it is predicted by 2140; all bitcoins will already be mined.

Thanks to its blockchain technology, you have ultimate control over your money and transactions without having to go through a third party such as the bank or PayPal.

Bitcoin transactions are also impossible to be reversed. Therefore, you should only deal with trusted parties as Bitcoin is also used as a means for cyber-crime like darknet markets or ransomware.

Media companies and investment firms in South Korea, India, Australia, and Japan have started discussing how Bitcoin may surpass the value of certain fiat currencies in the future as an alternative monetary system.

ABC News, a national news service in Australia have also reported recently it is likely for Bitcoin to replace even the USD in the next ten years if it sustains its current exponential growth.

The second most popular currency is **Ethereum.**

Created by Vitalik Buterin, it has scored itself the second spot in the hierarchy of cryptocurrencies. This digital currency launched in 2015 is predicted to surpass Bitcoin and may be the cryptocurrency of the future. Ethereum is currently worth $135 since its launch.

Is Ethereum similar to Bitcoin?
It is in a way, but not really. Like Bitcoin, Ethereum is a part of a blockchain network. The main difference between the two currencies is that Bitcoin blockchain focuses on tracking ownership of the digital currency while Ethereum blockchain focuses on running the programming code or network.

Instead of having to build an entirely original blockchain for each new application, Ethereum enables the development of thousands of different applications in a single platform. In the Ethereum blockchain, miners work to earn Ether. Ether is a crypto token that helps run the network.

Another use of the Ethereum blockchain is its ability to decentralize any services that are centralized. For instance, Ethereum is able to decentralize services like loans provided by banks, online transactions using PayPal as well as voting systems and much more.

Ethereum can also be used to build a Decentralized Autonomous Organization (DAO). A DAO is a fully autonomous organization without a leader. DAOs are run by programming codes on a collection of smart contracts written in the Ethereum blockchain. DAO is designed to replace the structure of a traditional organization and like Bitcoin, eliminating the need for people and centralized control.

What are the most apparent benefits of Ethereum?
Firstly, a third party cannot make any changes to the data. The system is also tamper and corruption proof. This is because Ethereum is built based on a network formed around a consensus. As a result, it is making censorship impossible.

Secondly, just like Bitcoin, Ethereum is backed up by secure cryptography. Therefore, the applications are well protected against any form of hacking.

The third cryptocurrency is **Litecoin**.

When the currency was first launched in 2011, it aspired to be the 'silver' to Bitcoin's 'gold.' Litecoin also recorded the highest market cap of any other mined cryptocurrency, after Bitcoin after its launch.

The main reason for Litecoin's creation is to make up what Bitcoin lacked. The main difference between Litecoin and Bitcoin is the 2.5-minute time to generate a block for Litecoin, as opposed to Bitcoin's 10 minutes.

For miners and technical experts, the Litecoin possesses a very important difference to Bitcoin, and that is a more improved work algorithm which speeds up the hashing power and system altogether.

One of the most significant advantages that Litecoin possesses is it can handle a higher volume of transactions thanks to its algorithm. The faster block time also prevents double-spending attacks.

While Litecoin failed to secure and maintain its second place after Bitcoin, it is still actively mined and traded and is bought by investors as a backup in case Bitcoin fails. The current value of Litecoin is $50.

The fourth currency is **Monero.**

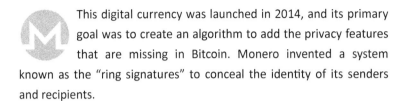

This digital currency was launched in 2014, and its primary goal was to create an algorithm to add the privacy features that are missing in Bitcoin. Monero invented a system known as the "ring signatures" to conceal the identity of its senders and recipients.

Ring signatures combine a user's private account keys with public keys obtained from Montero's blockchain to create a ring of possible signers that would not allow outsiders to link a signature to a specific user.

While Monero users can keep their transactions private, they are also able to share their information selectively. Every Monero account has a "view key," which allows anyone holding it to view the account's transactions.

Initially, the ring signature system concealed the senders and recipients involved in the Monero transactions without hiding the amount being transferred. However, an updated and improved version of the ring signature system known as "Ring CT" enabled the value of individual transactions as well as its recipients to be hidden.

Apart from ring signatures, Monero also improved its privacy settings by using "Stealth Addresses," which are randomly generated, one-time addresses.

These addresses are created for each transaction on behalf of the recipients.

With this feature, the recipients use a single address and transactions they receive go to separate, unique addresses. This way, Monero transactions cannot be linked to the published address of the recipients.

By providing a high level of privacy, Monero allows each unit of its currency to be exchanged between one another. Meaning, each of its coin has the same value.

Like the other cryptocurrencies, Monero offers interested parties to mine blocks. Individuals may choose to join a mining pool, or they may mine Monero by themselves.

Anyone with a computer can mine Monero, as they do not require

any specific hardware or specific integrated circuits like Bitcoin. Instead, Monero utilizes a Proof-of-Work (PoW) Algorithm that is designed to accept a wide range of processors, a feature which was included to ensure that mining was open to all parties.

The price of Monero has fluctuated quite frequently from its launch until May 2017, where the current value of the currency is now $43.80.

Monero has received the acceptance of multiple dark web marketplaces and has generated its fan base due to its privacy settings. Therefore, it is less speculative as compared to other digital currencies, and traders purchase Monero as a hedge for other cryptocurrencies.

Last but not least is **Ripple.**

Ripple is a technology that has a dual function; as a digital currency as well as a digital payment network for financial transactions. It was launched in 2012 and co-founded by Chris Larsen and Jed McCaleb. The cryptocurrency coin under Ripple is labeled as XRP.

Unlike the other cryptocurrencies, Ripple operates on an open-source and a peer-to-peer blockchain platform which allows a transfer of money in any form, both fiat, and cryptocurrency

Ripple uses a middleman in the currency transactions. The medium

(the middleman) known as "Gateway" acts as a link in the network between two parties wanting to make a transaction.

The way it works is that the Gateway functions as a credit intermediary that receives and sends currencies to public addresses over the Ripple network. This is why Ripple is less prevalent when compared to the other digital currencies, with only a $0.26 value to date.

Ripple's digital coin, XRP acts as a bridge for other currencies which includes both fiat and cryptocurrencies. In Ripple's network, any money can be exchanged between one another.

If user X wants Bitcoins as the form of payment for his services from Y, then Y does not necessarily have to possess Bitcoins. Y can pay X to X's Gateway using US Dollars or any other currencies. X will then receive Bitcoins converted from the US Dollars from his Gateway.

The nature of Ripple's network and it's systems exposes its users to certain risks. Even though you can exchange any currencies, the Ripple network does not run with a proof-of-work system like

Bitcoin. Instead, transactions are heavily reliant on a consensus protocol to validate account balances and operations on the system.

But Ripple does improve some features of traditional banks. Namely, transactions are completed within seconds on a Ripple network even though the system handles millions of transactions frequently.

Unlike traditional banks, even a wire transfer may take up days or weeks to complete. The fee to conduct transactions on Ripple is also very minimal, as opposed to large fees charged by banks to complete cross-border payments.

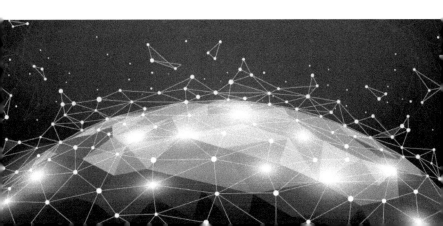

3

HOW TO OPEN AN ACCOUNT TO INVEST

To start investing in cryptocurrencies, the first thing you would need is to set up your digital wallet. In the cryptocurrency realm, the term used is "wallet." The portfolio can be likened to a bank account, which can be stored in different devices.

A cryptocurrency wallet is a software program that functions to store private and public keys and interacts with various blockchains. It enables users to send and receive cryptocurrencies as well as tracking their balance.

There are many wallets out there for you to choose from, which is all dependent on your security needs as well as whether you wish to be an active trader or a more passive buy-and-hold investor.

Once you have set up your wallet, you can then proceed to purchase and exchange the digital currency of your choice on many platforms. Firstly, let's explore the top 5 wallets for you to choose from to hold your crypto funds.

The top 5 wallets that you can choose from to store your cryptocurrencies are as follows:

- *BreadWallet.com*
- *Blockchain.info*
- *MyEtherWallet*
- *Jaxx Wallet*
- *Trezor*

Firstly, let's look at **BreadWallet.com.**

For now, bread wallet only receives Bitcoin to store in their digital wallets. This wallet is excellent for Bitcoin beginners as it is very user-friendly and straightforward to use. Most importantly, the tool is free to use.

All you need to do is to download bread wallet, choose a passcode and you are ready to receive your currencies. There are no login names or passwords and no complicated cryptographic keys or configuring any settings.

However, the downside of this wallet is that it can only be downloaded to your mobile device and there are no web or desktop interfaces. It also lacks features and it is a hot wallet, which means it has less security and other parties may access your private keys easier.

The second wallet is known as **Blockchain.info.**

Blockchain.info is catered towards Bitcoins only and is a mobile-based app for both iOS and Android. It also acts as a web-based wallet. The most distinguishable feature of Blockchain.info wallet is the newly developed payment channel for the Bitcoin network, known as "Thunder."

The technology enables users to send and receive Bitcoins without touching the main blockchain. This results in a very secure transaction and instant payments.

The Blockchain wallet is free and to create your account; you need to head to the main page and sign up for your account.

The third wallet is known as **MyEtherWallet.**

This wallet caters specifically to Ethereum currency. This wallet is user-friendly as it allows you to create a new wallet without having to download the blockchain as you can just use the web-based application.

MyEtherWallet is not your standard web wallet. It acts as an interface to directly interact with the Etherium blockchain. You do not have to create an account on their server. You just simply create a wallet which is yours to keep, where you may broadcast your transactions on the blockchain through their full node.

Next is the **Jaxx Wallet.**

The most significant advantage of Jaxx is that it supports many of the leading cryptocurrency platforms such as Bitcoin, Ethereum, Litecoin, Dash and many more. It is both available to be downloaded on the mobile device, or you can open it on the web.

It also has one of the best user interfaces as when you log in to the system you know how to navigate yourself, and it is pretty straightforward. They prioritize user experience.

Jaxx also has excellent security and privacy settings as your private keys are sent to your local device and never to any servers. This just means you have full access to your crypto funds and Jaxx does not hold or have access to any of your funds.

However, as the code is not an open source, the system sometimes can be quite slow to load.

Last but not least is **Trezor**

Trezor is a hardware Bitcoin wallet ideal for storing large amounts of Bitcoin. It is also suitable for beginners and very user-friendly and has perfect security and privacy settings. The web interface is easy to use, and the device comes with a built-in screen. Most importantly, it is open source software.

As it is a very secure and practical device, the cost is a little bit pricey at $99. You must also have a method to send your bitcoins.

We've already discussed the platforms where you can hold your cryptocurrencies. As mentioned previously, the wallets can be stored in different devices.

There are five types of devices where you can download and store your wallets to hold your cryptocurrencies:

- *Desktop*
- *Cloud*
- *Mobile Devices*
- *Hardware*
- *Paper*

Firstly, is your **desktop.**

Your wallets can be downloaded on a PC or laptop. They are only accessible from the single computer in which they are downloaded. It offers very good security, but the drawback is you are only able to access your wallet on the desktop and nowhere else.

The second drawback is when your PC is attacked by a virus; the virus may also affect your cryptocurrency wallet, and your wallet may get hacked. The virus may also access your private keys and your funds.

Secondly, your wallet can be downloaded and stored in the **cloud or**

online. The wallets run on the cloud and are accessible from any devices in any location.

They are very convenient to access unlike your wallets stored on the desktop. However, bear in mind that your private keys are stored online and other parties may potentially access your wallet quickly.

The next wallet is your mobile wallet. You can download your wallet on your mobile device via the App Store or Google Play store and others. Having your wallet on your mobile makes it very convenient as you have access to it anywhere you go.

A lot of them are quite secure as they have multiple signature accesses as well as backup features in case you lose your phone. This way you would not risk losing your crypto funds as the backup feature has backed up your private key to unlock your wallet.

The fourth wallet is your **hardware wallet.** A hardware wallet means you store your crypto funds on a USB or hard drive. Although hardware wallets complete their transactions online, they are stored offline, and this enhances the security.

Last but not least is you can store your wallet on paper. Paper wallets are wallets printed out on a piece of paper. They are very easy to use as you have the option to carry it wherever you go, or you can even store it somewhere safe.

Because they are printed out, they provide a very high level of security. While the term paper wallet can refer to a physical copy or printout of your public and private keys, it can also refer to a piece of software used to securely generate a pair of keys which are then printed.

Now this leaves us with an important question, where should you store your wallet which contains your crypto funds?

This all depends on whether you are an active or passive user of cryptocurrency. To asses which user you are, you need to answer the following questions:

- Do you need a wallet for everyday purchases, or just buying and holding your digital currency?
- Do you plan to use several currencies or just one single currency?
- Do you require access to your digital wallet wherever you are, even when you are on the go or only from home?

For instance, if you are the type of user who regularly spends your crypto funds to purchase daily necessities, you may want to store your wallet on your mobile device or the cloud.

 However, if you plan to buy and hold your currencies for future investments, it is best for you to store your wallet on a hardware or paper wallet.

Once you have chosen the best platform to hold your currencies, you can now proceed to the many digital currency exchanges to purchase your cryptocurrency and kick start your investment!

Cryptocurrency Exchanges for Investment

First and foremost, let's get familiar with cryptocurrency exchanges. What is a cryptocurrency exchange? Cryptocurrency exchanges are websites which allows you to buy, sell and exchange cryptocurrencies for other digital currency or fiat currencies like USD or Euro.

If you are very well versed in your crypto investment game and are used to trade professionally, you will likely need to use an exchange platform that requires you to open an account and verify your identity.

However, if you are relatively new to the realm of cryptocurrency as a beginner, I advise starting with platforms which do not require you to open an account.

These exchanges are usually very straightforward, and you can start occasionally trading until you get the hang of it.

There are three types of cryptocurrency exchanges:

Trading Platforms

These are websites that connect buyers and sellers where they charge certain fees for a completed transaction.

Direct Trading
These platforms offer a direct person to person exchange. You may exchange with individuals from different countries as well as different currencies. Direct trading does not necessarily adhere to the market price, as the individuals trading may set their exchange rate.

Brokers
These are websites that anyone can visit to purchase cryptocurrencies. However, the price is set by the broker. Cryptocurrency brokers are similar to foreign exchange dealers.

Before making your first trade, it's important to take note of these five essential pieces of information to minimize your risk and maximize your return on investment.

1. Reputation
> Before you start your exchange on your selected site, ensure you've gathered sufficient information regarding the location such as reviews from professional traders as well as popular industry websites. You may also join forums that discussescryptocurrency issues such as Bitcoin Talk or Reddit.

2. Fees

Most exchanges will have fee-related information on their websites. Before joining any sites, ensure you have under stood the exchange jargons; deposit, transaction and withdrawal fees. Fees may vary according to the exchange you choose.

3. Payment Methods

Take note of the payment method available. Does the site use credit and debit card? Wire transfer? PayPal? If a particular exchange has very limited payment methods, then it may not be convenient for you. Always remember that purchasing currencies via credit card will still require an ID verification and it comes with a premium price to increase the security measures.

Meanwhile, purchasing cryptocurrency via wire transfer will take longer as it takes time for banks to process.

4. Verification Requirements

Majority of Bitcoin's trading platforms both in the US and the UK require a form of ID verification to make deposits and withdrawals.

Some exchanges will also allow you to remain anonymous. Bear in mind that verifications may take up days, but this is protecting exchanges from any sort of money laundering.

5. Exchange Rate

Do not be surprised that different exchanges offer different rates. Therefore always remember to shop around and to not immediately settle on an exchange. This makes a big difference in your

investment as cryptocurrencies are known to fluctuate in value up to 10% and even higher in some circumstances.

As cryptocurrency is gaining more attention around the globe, there is a vast array of exchange platforms to choose from. But not all exchange platforms are created equal. These are the top 5 most visited exchange platforms in no particular order.

- Coinbase
- Kraken
- Cex.io
- ShapeShift
- Poloniex

Firstly, is **Coinbase.**

Coinbase is one of the most popular exchange platforms to date. It is used by trusted investors and millions of investors because it is FDIC insured up to $250,000. This platform is user-friendly as it makes it easy for you to buy, use, store and trade digital currency securely.

The platform allows you to exchange currencies like Bitcoin, Ethereum, and recently, Litecoin. They also have a digital wallet that is available on iPhone and Android.

However, the selection of tradable currencies is dependent on the country you live in. Currently, Coinbase only allows transactions in the US, Europe, UK, Canada, Australia, and Singapore. The method of payment is also quite limited and restricted to bank transfers, credit/ debit cards, and PayPal. To get started, all you need to do is to sign up for your account, and you are good to go!

The second platform is **Kraken.**

 Kraken is the largest Bitcoin exchange in euro volume and liquidity and is the first partner in the cryptocurrency bank. Kraken allows the exchange of Bitcoins, where you are also able to trade Bitcoins and euros, US Dollars, Canadian Dollars, British Pounds and Japanese Yen.

Kraken also allows the trade of other digital currencies such as Ethereum, Monero, Ethereum Classic, Augur REP tokens, Litecoin, ICONOMI, Zcash and many more.

Kraken also caters towards more experienced users where it offers margin trading and other advanced trading features. Cost wise, Kraken has very decent exchange rates, low transaction fees as well as minimal deposit fees.

However, like Coinbase, payment methods are also minimal. Kraken is also more suitable for advanced traders and investors, and it may be a little difficult for newcomers as it has an unintuitive user interface.

To open up a primary account to start trading, you need to sign up for your account on their main page where it requires your personal details. A more advanced account additionally requires a government-issued ID and proof of residence.

The third exchange platform is **Cex.io**.

This platform enables its users to easily trade fiat currency with cryptocurrencies and vice versa. For traders looking to trade Bitcoins professionally, the platform offers personalized and user-friendly trading dashboards and margin trading.

CEX also offers a brokerage service which provides inexperienced traders an effortless way to purchase Bitcoins according to the market rate. CEX is a convenient mobile product where it is supported worldwide and has a very decent exchange rate. However, depositing currencies in your account are quite expensive.

To start your trading on CEX, you need to head on to the main page and sign up for your account.

Next up is **ShapeShift.**

ShapeShift is tailored towards users who wish to make instant straightforward trades without signing up for an account or relying on a platform to hold your funds.

It also supports the exchange of multiple cryptocurrencies including Bitcoin, Ethereum, Monero, Zcash and many more. However, it does not allow fiat currency exchange with cryptocurrencies and the payment methods are very limited as users are not allowed to purchase their digital currencies with debit/credit cards or any other payment system. Payments are to be done via cryptocurrencies only.

Last but not least is **Poloniex.**

This platform offers a secure trading environment with more than 100 different Bitcoin cryptocurrency pairings and advanced features for professional investors.

Poloniex has a fee schedule for all its traders. Therefore, the fee that is charged varies depending on if you are a maker or a taker. Makers are traders who display their orders on order prior to the trade. Takers are users who "takes" the makers order.

For makers, their fees range from 0 to 0.15% depending on the amount traded. For takers, fees range from 0.10 to 0.25%. The reason why the prices vary is that the maker-taker model encourages market liquidity by rewarding the makers of that liquidity with a fee discount.

To start trading, you have to sign up for an account on Poloniex's main page.

To start investing, you have to first possess a digital wallet. Then, shop around for suitable exchange platforms according to your preferences. The main factor to take into account before starting your investment is to acknowledge whether you are an active or passive user of cryptocurrency; are you in it for the short-term, or the long-run?

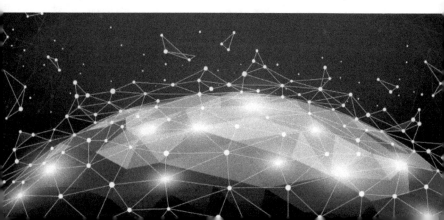

4

STRATEGIES TO INVEST

Investing in cryptocurrencies comes with its own risks as well as rewards. Therefore, you need to invest strategically to maximize your return on investment and minimize your risks. There are specific strategies you need to adopt to ensure a successful cryptocurrency investment and building your portfolio.

There are 5 strategies, which may come in handy for you especially if you are relatively new to the cryptocurrency realm.

1. *Understand the whole concept of cryptocurrency*
2. *Spy on the market*
3. *Invest in more than one coin*
4. *Start small and scale higher*
5. *Reallocate your investment*
6. *Research the projects/currencies*

Firstly, it is crucial for you to understand the whole concept of cryptocurrency.

Always keep in mind that you do not merely invest in something you are not sure and uncertain of. Do not jump on the bandwagon and follow what other people are doing just because you fear of missing out. For instance, a lot of people see their peers investing in property, and they follow suit in hopes to generate millions without even conducting prior research.

Therefore, the first thing you ought to do is to study the space. These are the important points to be digested before kick-starting your investment:

- What is cryptocurrency?
- What is Blockchain Technology?
- What is Bitcoin?
- What are the other popular digital currencies?
- What are the coins market caps?
- How can you start your own cryptocurrency exchanges?
- Where can you make cryptocurrency exchanges?

Take your time to understand the realm of cryptocurrency and don't rush the process. It may take weeks or even months to digest all the information, but this step is imperative for you so you can be on top of the game and an expert in the field. This way, there's a meager chance for you to waste your resources as you are familiar with the cryptocurrency industry.

 The second strategy to invest is to spy on the market.

What does spying on the market mean? Spying on the market says you are observing what is currently working in the cryptocurrency market. What you want to look into specifically is:

- What is the most sought-after currency?
- What is the value of the currency?
- Which currency has the highest market cap?
- Should you buy and hold the currency for future
- investments?

Always remember that the cryptocurrency market is very volatile and the values fluctuate now and then. The benefits usually depend on a lot of factors such as the speculators, the market demand, the supply-demand and different institutions manipulating the prices.

My advice is for you to shop around and do not settle immediately for a specific cryptocurrency just because it has the highest value or popularity at the moment.

For instance, the most sought-after currency at the moment is Bitcoin, but many professional traders and investors have predicted that Ethereum may surpass Bitcoin and become the currency of the future in the coming years. Therefore, always spy on the market and analyze the information.

The next strategy is to invest in more than one cryptocurrency.

It is not wise to invest all of your money into a single digital currency. A well-balanced portfolio minimizes your risk as when you possibly lose on a cryptocurrency you own, you can still gain with the other ones you have. If you decide to invest in only one currency, for example, Litecoin, what if the whole currency collapses? You'll lose all of the money you have invested in a split second without any backups.

Therefore, always invest in 2 or more currencies. Constantly spy on the market and choose the currency you prefer.

The fourth strategy is to start small and scale higher as you go.

A lot of people assume you become instantly rich when you invest in cryptocurrency. However, that is not always the case. You don't just become rich once you choose to invest in cryptocurrency. There are a strategy and a learning curve to get where you want to be. Therefore, always remember to start small, especially for those who have a small risk appetite. As mentioned in the previous chapters,

cryptocurrency values are very volatile as it depends on many factors. The costs fluctuate even more in this cryptocurrency season where many people are starting to trade digital currencies.

For beginners, the rule of thumb is to start investing $500 for your cryptocurrencies. You don't necessarily have to start investing thousands! Now that you have your $500, how do you divide the  money and what currency do you begin to purchase first?

Firstly, remember to sign up for your digital wallet, and deposit your fiat currency and purchase the top 2 cryptocurrencies; Bitcoin and Ethereum. The reason why we're selecting the 2 is that they are the safest and established choice as compared to the other currencies. They are prone to fluctuation, but not as much for now and they are called king currencies.

So, you split the $500, and purchase $250 worth of Bitcoin and $250 for Ethereum. This is a smart way to do it, and if there are chances of you losing any of your funds, the risk is still worth taking. When you get the hang of it, you can scale your investment higher by purchasing your cryptocurrencies in a higher value.

Last but not least is to reallocate your investment.

Once you've completed all the steps from 1-4, which means you're familiar with the cryptocurrency realm, you can reallocate your funds according to the digital currency market. When you've started trading and investing, you'll notice over a while some currencies will do better than others.

For instance, you've observed Bitcoin's market, and it has gone up whereas Ethereum has gone down, you can drag your funds to the higher currency market. This means, you can play around according to what's working in the current market and constantly reallocate your money.

When you get the hang of it, you'll realize that your investment will build up eventually from $500 to $1000, from $1000 to possibly $100,000! Always remember to do your part in getting to know more of the cryptocurrency market as there is still something new to look into. Be strategic in your investment and only investment in what you know!

5

HOW TO COLLECT MORE BITCOIN

There are six methods for you to earn more Bitcoins and it is not only restricted to cryptocurrency exchange or trading. The six modes are:

1. *Cryptocurrency exchange*
2. *Faucets*
3. *Micro-tasking*
4. *Supplying Bitcoin-related services*
5. *Becoming a Bitcoin Escrow Agent*
6. *Bitcoin Affiliate Marketing*

The first method to collect more Bitcoins is by cryptocurrency exchange or trading.

As mentioned in the previous modules, there are various forms of trading or exchange options available for Bitcoin. You may trade Bitcoin for Bitcoin, or Bitcoin with other cryptocurrencies, and even Bitcoin with fiat currencies.

But most importantly, ensure you have equipped yourself with the knowledge required to start exchanging Bitcoin, so you know the risks involved as well as how much you need to invest as a beginner.

One of the most common ways of accumulating and earning Bitcoin through trading is by "Day Trading." Day trading is the buying and selling of Bitcoins on the same day, based on small, short-term price fluctuations.

Therefore, when you observe the market and notice that the value of Bitcoin is going up, it's an excellent time to purchase some Bitcoins and sell them right away after you've made your profit.

The second method to earn Bitcoins is through "Faucets."

What are Faucets?

Faucets are websites which give away Bitcoins regularly. They may give away Bitcoins every minute, every 10 minutes, every hour or once a week. All you need to do is to sign up on the websites using your Bitcoin address and sometimes your email. And if you are selected, you get the Bitcoins.

However, one downside to this method is the amount of Bitcoin given away is not as much, and sometimes the most you'll get is 0.00288BTC which equals to $1.31. But still, who would want to give you Bitcoins for free? And looking at how volatile the cryptocurrency market is, it is definitely worth the try!

Some of the popular Faucets that you can try to sign up to win your

- Bitcoins are:
- Bitcoin Zebra
- Moon Bitcoin
- Weekend Bitcoin
- Milli

The third method to earn your Bitcoin is by micro-tasking.

Micro-tasking is websites that pay their users using Bitcoins for completing tasks such as filling up surveys, watching videos and signing up for new services. You can sign up for free, and all the functions can be done within your own time! One example of a micro-tasking site is Coinworker.

Next, you can earn Bitcoin by offering Bitcoin-related services.

Not many people know that you can get paid with Bitcoin instead of Fiat Currency for offering Bitcoin-related services. If you want to get an idea of what services you could provide you with can visit Coinality, a site which gives current updates on Bitcoin jobs posted online.

You can also visit BitcoinTalk, a forum which discusses a wide range of cryptocurrency topics, including a services thread where users are searching for Bitcoin service providers.

Some examples of services people are looking for are:

- *Blockchain developer*
- *Website manager*
- *Graphic designer*
- *Mining expert*
- *Online marketer*
- *Writing for cryptocurrency blogs and news sites*

The fifth method for you to earn more Bitcoin is by becoming a Bitcoin Escrow agent.

What is a Bitcoin Escrow Agent?

An agent handles the 3rd party escrow service of a Bitcoin  transaction. Bitcoin escrow agents are getting more and more common as escrow protects users from fraudulent buyers by requiring the Bitcoin to be deposited upfront. Usually, Bitcoin transactions are anonymous exchanges that involve untrusted parties.

In an event where the sellers turn out to be scammers, the escrow agent will act as an arbitrator and determines who will receive the Bitcoins. Many Bitcoin marketplaces provide escrow services, such as LocalBitcoins, CryptoThrift, and BitPremier. To be an escrow agent, you must build up your reputation as a trustworthy party in the community.

Last but not least is getting involved in Bitcoin affiliate marketing.

For those who are not familiar with affiliate marketing, the idea behind it is that you promote someone else's product and they pay you a percentage of the profit based on the sales you bring in.

Let's illustrate an example. Let's say you decide to promote TREZOR, a hardware cryptocurrency wallet. If a person chooses to purchase TREZOR and the customers came from your site, you get a commission for it.

I've already listed the possible methods to earn your Bitcoins. Always remember whatever way you choose to venture into, there's no such thing as easy money. If earning Bitcoins were that easy, everyone would have done it by now.

In each of the methods listed above, you will either need to invest your time or your money. There is no easy way out. Try what works for you and be patient with the results.

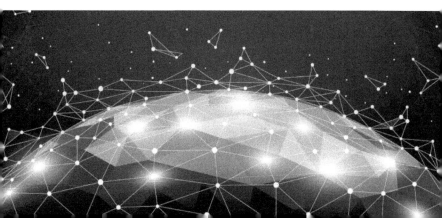

6

Like most things' tech, the realm of cryptocurrency can be a bit complex to master and is still new to many. But the advantage of purchasing this currency is undoubtedly worth your investment in both time and money. Experts have also predicted that it may be the next big thing in finance.

As a digital asset that serves users online, Cryptocurrency has many appealing benefits. Some of this is thanks to the Blockchain Technology previously mentioned. It is a strictly monitored process with encrypted transaction and control thus, making this online money a thing for the future.

So, in this chapter, we will cover the top **4 benefits of Cryptocurrency.**

The most well-known benefit of this investment is its **'No Third-Party Involvement.'** There's always a pattern when using traditional money to buy yourself a new property, setting up your own business, or buying a new car.

One way or another, the process requires a third-party involvement. We are talking lawyers, owners, and some other external factors such as delays, documentations, and extra fees. This, in general, will consume unnecessary time, money and energy to the point of giving up.

An excellent example of this scenario would be you buying a new house. You need to pay the Financial Advisor who in general, advises your financial statement to ensure you have a stable income.

Some property requires you to pay for a booking fee to 'lock' your house of choice and many other add-ons. In short, there's a lot of third-involvement, and it charges you even before you own the property.

But that is not the case with Cryptocurrency. As mentioned previously, the blockchain system is similar to a self-rights database.

It means, the contract is capable of being design and enforces to

remove any involvement of the third-party mentioned before. Moreover, the agreement can be customized to complete a particular transaction at a set date at a fraction of any expenses.

Yes, you can eliminate any third-party involvement options you don't even need one. In short, you are in control of your own money using Cryptocurrency. This is what we call the 'Decentralized' system, which means there's no 'Central or Federal Government' regulating it for  you. Your transaction is practically immune to any influence from your government and its distinct manipulation.

So, it is possible to be able to pay and receive money anywhere in the world at any given time. That transaction is done with minimum processing fees, thus preventing users from having to pay extra charges from banks or any financial institutions.

Next advantage would be **the risk it holds is lower than traditional currencies.**

In this era, most people rarely have their cash in their possession now. Instead, they have an array of credit cards, debit cards and other payment cards available as their nations' method of payment.

Nothing's wrong with that, except however if the store's connection to the server is disconnected or their machine is out of service, and

you who do not possess any cash just ended up holding the line. The thing about these cards are, any purchase you are making, you are giving the end-receiver access to your full-credit line. No matter how small the amount of the transaction is, the fact that you are giving someone your card to gain access to your account is already a form of 'breach.'

Most of this 'breach' is considered secure nowadays using differing safety measures like 'PIN enabled' or 'Pay wave' methods.

Then, the store initiates payment by 'pulling' the designated amount from your account using the information provided within your card.

Cryptocurrency doesn't work that way. Instead of a 'pulling' mechanisms, it 'pushes' the amount that is needed to be pay or receive to other cryptocurrency holders without any further information needed.

Payments are possible without your personal information being tied to you the transaction. Your account can be backed up and encrypted to ensure the safety of your money.

By allowing users to be in control of their transactions helps keep Bitcoin, Ether or other distinguished cryptocurrencies safe for the network.

Another benefit of using Cryptocurrency would be its **protection from fraud.**

We often heard cases where other users but not the owner are using one's payment card. When contacting his card's service issuer, it is found that the card has made certain transactions without his

consent. This is what we call a fraud case.

Most of the time these fraud cases get away with the crime because it is not easy to trace the fraud back to the perpetrator. What's more, it is even trying to get the attention  of law enforcer to launch an investigation with only a single instance of crime the perpetrator commits.

However, Cryptocurrency is not viable to fraud act. Because your personal information is kept hidden under unnecessary prying eyes, this protects you against identity theft.

Remember, a Cryptocurrency is a form of digital money, created from code. Individual cryptocurrencies are as mentioned, digital, and cannot be counterfeited by senders.

Because the transactions cannot be reversed, they do not carry with them any personal information. This ensures security and the merchants are protected from any potential losses that might occur from fraud cases.

It is tough to cheat or making false pose on anyone using these Cryptocurrencies due to its decentralized system and the existing blockchain system. It cannot be manipulated by anyone or organization thanks to it being cryptographically secure.

Lastly would be its **Universality.**

Throughout payment history, nations worldwide have their differing methods of payments implemented. We have money-goods exchange system and even bartering trade. It is not until traders visited other countries that they found out how to trade items to one another.

Thanks to various innovations and developments, we now have multiple methods to trade and exchange sums of money worldwide.

But even with all the upgrades, we are still experiencing problems doing transactions across the globe. There are always currency issues, bank authorizations, unacceptable payment method and some other varying issues encountered by business owners or travelers out there.

Fact is, not all country has similar financial processions. Your card or currency may not be accepted by other countries, and that is a major setback to your account.

For example, most online banking, payment or cash system requires additional processing fees for their service even if that account is yours.

However, Cryptocurrencies are not bound by any of those exchange rates, transaction charges, the interest rates or any other fees applied to many countries.

They can be used at any time at any international standard without experiencing any problems. It also saves a lot of your time and money by reducing additional spending over transferring money from multiple countries to another.

Which means cryptocurrency operates at an international platform which in turns, make the transaction easier than your average telegraphic transfer.

To recap, there are four significant advantages concerning Cryptocurrencies. It has 'No Third-Party Involvement,' 'Lower Risk compared to Traditional Currencies,'

'Protection from Fraud' and 'Universality.'

Despite the fantastic advantages that come with Cryptocurrencies, there are also some setbacks to this investment. We will uncover it in the next chapter.

7

ARE THERE ANY DRAWBACKS?

Previously, it was mentioned how Cryptocurrency is one of a kind of digital currency without likeness. Because not many payments nowadays are without the involvement of a third-party, lower risk payment, little to no fraud cases and most of all, universal in its usage.

However, considering the online nature of Cryptocurrency, some flaws come with it. There are 4 major setbacks concerning Cryptocurrency.

The first one is the **lack of understanding over Cryptocurrency.**

In most cases, people are still unaware of the digital currency world and the potential it holds.

This is similar to when the usage of the credit card was first announced, and the reception towards it is relatively similar to Cryptocurrency. Back then, people wouldn't even think that paying things using a small card is possible, what's more using a whole new digital currency.

Because it is different, and it doesn't involve cash directly, people shy away from it and continuously doubting its effectiveness. Additionally, it requires online access to make it work.

The idea of having to pay things or transfer money online is convenient to some, but most are still skeptical about it.

To make Cryptocurrency acceptable around us, the people need to be educated about it to be able to include it in their daily lives. One way to do it is through networking. But the fact is, there are not many places online where people can learn about it.

The effort to learn a whole new world of currency requires a lot of time and energy. Most would think it is not worth their time because it is not commonly known anyway.

Even though some businesses are accepting bitcoins, the list is significantly small compared to traditional currencies.

This is probably due to the lack of knowledgeable staff that understands the ways of digital currencies. Plus, they need to help educate their customer about it and how to use it for a smooth transaction. This, again, will take a longer time and effort to teach others.

Another drawback of Cryptocurrency would be its **lack of protection and guarantee.**

In the case of traditional currency, there's Central Bank who governs the authority on every nation's money. No higher power can suddenly decide that they no longer want to use their country's currency to trade without protest and rejection.

There are proceedings to follow, documents to file, approvals, and many other protocols to support. However, that is not the case with our digital currency. There is no  Central Bank who governs Bitcoin, which means no one can guarantee its minimum valuation.

The value of Bitcoin, for example, will fall tremendously should a significant group of merchants decided to just 'discard' Bitcoins and leave the system. This will inevitably put other users who have invested thousands of dollars into Bitcoins into a major loss. There is no one to contact to file these losses, or rules to help compensate it.

Thus, the decentralized system of Bitcoin is what we call a

double-edged sword on its own.

The next disadvantage is its **technical shortcomings.**

When online banking made its way to our life, there's always a risk of a sudden server failure, power shortage, and even hardware lags.

If it happens and you ended up getting a charge but didn't receive the online movie tickets or flight tickets, you can always call bank service provider, or go to the physical bank instead and declares your case.

Most of the cases if you show evidence of your payment you will get proper compensations or feedbacks.

That is not how it works with Cryptocurrency. First of all, this currency does not have a bank to negotiate and help you around. There is no fixed number that you could call and ask for clarification.

So, if you bought your goods using Bitcoins for example, and the merchant didn't send the items you purchased, there is nothing you can do to reverse the transaction or refund. You can't complain about it to the police or any relating authority for that matter.

BLUE ARROW ABSTRACT

Similar to data corruptions or virus infections, if your hard drive crashes and your wallet file is corrupted your Bitcoin is lost forever. There is nothing you can you do restore it and those 'coins' will be 'orphaned' in the system.

The last major disadvantage of Cryptocurrency would be because it is **still developing.**

When things are still developing, it is prone to many risks. There are so many incomplete features that can be improved, but it takes a longer time to finalize it, especially if it has no physical form.

With traditional currency, despite the method of payments

nowadays are done online, and without us seeing the physical money transferring from one account to another, in the end of the day, when you reach the ATM, you are capable of holding that cash.

You can use it to buy stuff from the stores physically, and online. That shows how developed our traditional currency is.

Since Cryptocurrency does not have any physical forms, its usage is apparently restricted. It must always be converted to traditional currency to enjoy its worth. According to studies, there was a time when there is a proposition to store Bitcoin wallet information in cards. However, there is neither consensus nor continuation of the proposal.

Most probable reason would be because merchants find it unfeasible to support all the cryptocurrency cards. There is no system for an immediate payment using the cards. Thus users are forced to convert it into real money anyway.

As you can see, there are four disadvantages of Cryptocurrencies. There is a lack of understanding of this digital currency. Plus, there's minimum protection and guarantee when using it. Because it is mostly operating online, it is bound to experience all kinds of technical flaws, and it is still developing.

The world of cryptocurrency is relatively new to some people, and it can be difficult to understand. Because nobody knows what currencies will or can be adopted and at what scale.

So, in the next chapter, we will talk about what the future holds for Cryptocurrency.

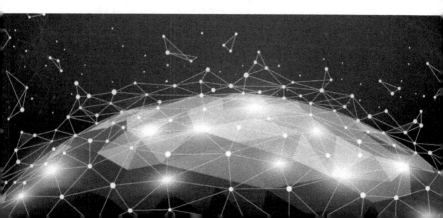

8

THE FUTURE OF CRYPTOCURRENCY

Now we will finally touch upon the future of Cryptocurrency.

These digital currencies have been said to be able to capture the world of online finance. With the blockchain technology behind it, the future of Cryptocurrency is showing a prosperous potential.

Starting in 2017, the alternative currencies will need to watch their prices closer than usual. Studies show that Bitcoin experienced a drop in its price. It seems like a cheaper cryptocurrency by the name Ether, reached its highest at $40 a unit. That's right.

Although the mechanism behind Ether prevents it from being used as a direct payment method, this cryptocurrency seems to have a brighter future ahead. This is all thanks to its clever contract concepts.

On the other hand, cryptocurrencies who are concerned over privacy are starting to gain more prominent favor amongst users.

Bitcoin, unfortunately despite their security measures, it continues to have loopholes that can be exploited for access to users' data. But this doesn't stop users from investing in Bitcoin. Up to this day, Bitcoin is still being accepted as a means of payment.

The level of acceptance is clearly bringing this alternative currency to the mainstream. Some companies are genuinely considering to invest in this currency, further fueling its journey to the world of financial currency. Are we going to witness a new norm of currency by cryptocurrency one day? Researchers concluded that it is still too early to predict that it would, but one thing is for sure that this currency is slowly making its way to the world.

The most targeted group of all would be the technologically savvy individuals and most of us are already part of this group. More than 50% of our time is spent online and it won't be long until it reaches a hundred....

...one day, we might even consider
using Cryptocurrency as our standard
currency for a more universal transaction.

51% attack – One of the ways to disrupt a cryptocurrency's blockchain is to control more than 51% of the network. This requires massive computing power and while possible on paper, the resources, coordination and finances required to do this would make it almost impossible to achieve. In this case, a 51% attack is only theoretical.

A

Address – a string of alphanumeric characters that represent a destination or origin from when and to cryptocurrencies are sent – all addresses are unique.

Airdrop – A method of distributing cryptocurrency amongst a population, first attempted with Auroracoin in early 2014.

Algorithm – a set of mathematical instructions or rules that need to be followed in problem solving. For example, there exists various algorithms to solve a rubix cube. If the algorithm is applied correctly, the outcome is that the cube is solved.

Altcoin – (Alternative coin) – A collective name given to all other cryptocurrencies that are not bitcoin. These include Ethereum, Golem, MOnero, Ripple, Dash, Litecoin, Dogecoin, Reddcoin, StratisCoin, Blackcoin, yocoin and MANY MANY others. There are over 700 recognized cryptocurrencies, tokens and assets today.

AML – Anti-Money Laundering laws are a series of regulations designed to prevent money being converted from criminal activity to what appear to be legitimate assets.

Angel Investor – A wealthy individual who provides startup businesses with capital in exchange for debt or equity in the business.

Arbitrage – The generation of risk free profits by trading between markets which have different prices for the same asset.

ASIC – A computer processing chip that is designed to perform 1 function and 1 function only. Most modern computers have multi-thread CPU's that allow the computer to complete a range of tasks all at the same time, whereas an ASIC computer focusses only on 1 function. In the crypto space, an ASIC computer is used to mine Bitcoin.

ASIC Miner – A computer that contains an Application Specific Integrated Circuit chip that are used to mine for bitcoins. They may connect directly to a computer or network wirelessly or with the use of an ethernet cable.

B

Bear Trap – This is a manipulation of a stock or commodity by investors. Traders who "set" the bear trap do so by selling stock until it fools other investors into thinking its upward trend in value has stopped, or is dropping. Those who fall into the bear trap will often sell at that time, fearing a further drop in value. At that point, the investors who set the trap will buy at the low price and will release the trap—which is essentially a false bear market. Once the bear trap is released, the value will even out, or even climb.

Bear market – A market that is in a downtrend (prices are going down) The term relates to the direction that a bear attacks. (Bears attack by swiping downwards with their claws.)

Bit – A unit of information expressed as either a 0 or 1 in binary notation. Bit is also used regarding Bitcoin as a common unit used to designate a sub-unit of a bitcoin – 1,000,000 bits is equal to 1 bitcoin. This unit is more convenient for pricing tips, goods and services.

Bitcoin – Bitcoin was founded in 2009 and is the most widely used crypto currency. It was supposedly created by the mysterious Satoshi Nakamoto, whose true identity is unknown and has yet to be verified. Bitcoin is not controlled by a centralized government or agency. The Bitcoin network is designed to mathematically generate no more than 21 million Bitcoins and was designed regulate itself to deal with inflation.

Bitcoin Protocol – The open source, cryptographic protocol which operates on the Bitcoin network, setting the "rules" for how the network runs.

Bitcoin Network – The decentralized, peer-to-peer network which maintains the blockchain. This is what processes all Bitcoin transactions.

Bitcoin (unit of currency) – 100,000,000 satoshis. A unit of the decentralized, digital currency which can be traded for goods and services. Bitcoin also functions as a reserve currency for the altcoin ecosystem.

BitcoinJS – An online library of JavaScript code used for Bitcoin development, particularly web wallets. *bitcoinjs.org*

BitcoinQT – Bitcoin QT is an open source software client used by your computer. It contains a copy of the blockchain and once installed it turns your computer into a node in the Bitcoin Network. Also acts as a "desktop wallet".

Bitcoin Days Destroyed – An estimate for the "velocity of money" within the Bitcoin network. This is used because it gives greater weight to bitcoins that have not been spent for a long time, and better represents the level of economic activity taking place with bitcoin than total transaction volume per day.

Block – Blocks are digital files where data pertaining to a cryptocurrency network is permanently recorded. A block records some or all of the most recent transactions that have not yet entered any prior blocks. Thus a block is like a page of a ledger or record book. Each time a block is 'completed', it gives way to the next block in the blockchain. A block is thus a permanent store of records which, once written, cannot be altered or removed.

Blockchain – A series of linked databases which form the backbone of the Bitcoin backbone. It is a digital ledger in which transactions made in bitcoin are recorded chronologically and publicly.

Block explorer – a search engine for a cryptocurrency, block explorers allow you to query transactions, addresses and other information.

Block height – the number of completed blocks in the blockchain.

Block reward – The coins that are paid to the computer (or pool of computers that finds a working hash to complete a block in the mining process of cryptocurrencies.

Bollinger Bands – Bands that use historical data in a market to indicate possibly volatility.

BTC – BTC is a common unit used to designate one bitcoin.

Bull Market – A market that is in an uptrend. (Prices are going up) The term relates to the direction in which a bull attacks (horns low to the ground, a bull strikes upwards)

C

Confirmation – All transactions on the blockchain need to be verified by all nodes – each verification of the transaction is called a confirmation.

Consensus – Consensus is achieved when all participants of the network agree on the validity of the transactions, ensuring that databases are exact copies of each other.

Crypto Currency – A cryptocurrency is a digital or virtual currency that uses advanced cryptography for security. A cryptocurrency is difficult to counterfeit because of this security feature. A defining feature of a cryptocurrency, and arguably its most endearing allure, is its organic nature; it is not issued by any central authority, rendering it theoretically immune to government interference or manipulation.

Cryptography – The process of using codes and ciphers to encrypt and decrypt sensitive information, messages or data.

D

Dapp – decentralized application that exists on a blockchain. Dapps are renowned for having proven 100% uptime.

Darksend – Darksend is Darkcoin's decentralized implementation, which was designed to give users of Darkcoin greater transactional privacy/anonymity.

DAO – Decentralized Autonomous Organizations – A blockchain technology inspires organization or corporation that exists and operates without human intervention.

DDoS – Abbreviation for Distributed Denial of Service. A DDoS is a cyber attack utilizing many different computers to tie up the resources of a website or web service. Some Bitcoin exchanges have come under DDoS attacks.

DDos Attack – An attack on a server or network intended to suspend or interrupt the services it provides. Stands for "distributed denial of service" attack. This is done by overwhelming it with traffic from multiple sources.

Deepweb – The content online not indexed by search engines making it difficult to access. The majority of content on the internet resides on the deepweb and can be accessed using a program called TOR. This is also where illegal sites such as Silk Road exist.

Deflation – A decrease in the general price level of goods in an economy. Traditionally this has taken place when a currency's demand collapses, however it is a natural property of bitcoin.

Demurrage – Certain currencies penalize users for hoarding, this is done via demurrage, where a fee is charged for holding unspent coins. This fee increases as time passes.

Desktop Wallet – A wallet that stores the private keys on your computer, which allow the spending and management of your bitcoins.

Deterministic Wallet – A wallet based on a system of deriving multiple keys from a single starting point known as a seed. This seed is all that is needed to restore a wallet if it is lost and can allow the creation of public addresses without the knowledge of the private key.

Difficulty – A measure of the amount of computing power required to solve the hash of a block. This is what increases to counteract increasing network hashrate in order to maintain a 10 minute confirmation time; re-adjusts every 2016 blocks.

Double Spending – The act of spending the same bitcoins twice. The blockchain plus bitcoin mining exist to confirm all transactions and to prevent such fraud.

Dust Transactions – Transactions so small that they are considered "spam" by the network. They are not relayed to stop people accidentally or deliberately clogging the blockchain.

E

Escrow – The practice of having a third party act as an intermediary in a transaction. This third party holds the funds on and sends them off when the transaction is completed.

ETF – Acronym for "Exchange Traded Fund". These are investment funds traded on stock markets that track the price index of an underlying asset.

Exchange – A central platform for exchanging different forms of cryptocurrencies and. Typically, bitcoin exchanges are used to exchange cryptocurrency for traditional monetary units.

F

Faucet – A website which gives away free bitcoins or other cryptocurrency to any IP address that connects to them.

Fiat Currency – Fiat currency is money that a government has declared legal tender by fiat (order or decree). It is not backed up by any physical or tangle commodity (something that can be bought or sold). It's value is strictly established by supply and demand. The US Dollar, British Pound, Euro, etc. are fiat currencies which became so after the abolishment of the gold standard.

FOMO – Fear Of Missing Out – A mindset that causes people to purchase a stock based on the premise that they may miss out on a good thing.

Fork – a split resulting in a new (updated) version of the original cryptocurrency. Happens when there is a major update that requires a new version of software to be implemented.

FUD – Fear, Uncertainty and Doubt – Rumours and misinformation that can have an affect on a stock or a crypto that causes people to sell their holdings. Sometimes distributed deliberately to cause confusion and lend an advantage to those who start the spread of information.

Frictionless – In reference to payment systems, a system is "frictionless" when there are zero transaction costs or restraints on trading.

G

Genesis Block – The first block in the blockchain.

GPU – Acronym for "graphics processing unit" is a specialized processor originally designed for the high graphics requirements of computer games. These are also used to mine cryptocurrency since they outperform CPUs.

H

Halving – Every 4 years, the "reward" for successfully mining a block of bitcoin is reduced by half. This is referred to as "Halving". For instance, the initial reward for mining a BitCoin Block was 50 BitCoins, which was reduced to 25 in 2012 after the first "halving" and half again to 12.25 bitcoins after the next halving. This mechanism ensures a finite amount of coins are created for a crypto currency. The actual time span is not 4 years, but rather the amount of time taken to mine 210 000 blocks.

Hard Fork – A complete change to the protocol used for a particular cryptocurrency. It is a complete divergence from the previous software version of the Blockchain for a cryptocurrency, and nodes running previous versions will no longer be accepted by the newest version.

Hash – A hash is a mathematical process that converts inputted data into a fixed length string, usually 32 characters. In the world of bitcoin, a hash must follow certain rules and formats and is formulated using very specific information, and must contain the previous hash and block information within itself together with some "dummy data" (a nonce) to produce a randomized hash. Not all hashes will be accepted. Even the slightest modification of the original input data would result in a completely different hash. A hash is "rehashed" thousands of times over per second until a suitable hash is found. The hash is created by the computers trying to find a suitable hash out of hundreds of thousands. Once a hash is created, it is then stored at the end of the blockchain. The computer that is responsible for submitting a working hash is allocated a reward in the form of bitcoin.

Hash Rate – This is the measuring unit of the processing power of the whole Bitcoin network. The network must make difficult mathematical operations for the purpose of security. For example, when we speak about a hashrate of 1 Th/s, it means you are producing 1 trillion calculations per second.

I

Inflation – An increase in the general price level of goods in an economy.

Inputs – This is a reference to an output of a previous transaction. Inputs to an address are added up, and this amount determines the amount a wallet can spend in outputs.

K

Kimoto Gravity Well – A mining difficulty readjustment algorithm, which was created in 2013 for Megacoin, an altcoin. The well allows difficulty readjustment to occur every block, instead of every 2016 blocks for Bitcoin. This was done as a response to concern about multi pool mining schemes.

KYC – Acronym for "Know Your Customer", used to describe a series of laws and regulations which require businesses to know the identity of their customers.

L

Laundry – Also known as a "mixing service", they combine funds from various users and redistribute them, making tracing the bitcoins back to their original source very difficult by mixing their "taint".

Leverage – Often used to describe trading with borrowed capital (margin) in order to increase the potential return of an investment.

Trading with "borrowed" bitcoins/money.

Litecoin – One of the first notable "altcoins". Created by Bobby Lee to be a "silver to bitcoin's gold". Litecoin uses the Scrypt mining algorithm instead of SHA256, has a 2.5 minute confirmation times, and has a total coin supply of 84 million coins.

Liquidity – The availability of an asset to be bought and sold easily, without affecting its market price.

Liquidity Swap – As a financial instrument on cryptocurrency exchanges, liquidity swaps are contracts where investors offer loans to others to trade with in exchange for a set return.

M

Margin Trading – The trading of assets or securities bought with borrowed money. A trader usually contributes an initial amount which is then used as collateral for their debt.

Market Order – A buy or sell order which gets executed at whatever the market price is at the time.

Merged Mining – This allows a miner to work on multiple blockchains simultaneously, contributing to the hash rate (and thus security) of both currencies being mined. E.g. Namecoin has implemented merged mining with Bitcoin.

Micro-transaction – A financial transaction involving small to tiny sums of money. Traditionally amounts under a dollar have been impractical due to transaction fees, however, cryptocurrencies have potential to change this.

mBTC – A bitcoin metric of 1 thousandth of a bitcoin (0.001 BTC).

Mining – Bitcoin mining is the process by which transactions are verified and added to the public ledger, known as the block chain, and also the means through which new bitcoin are released. Anyone with access to the internet and suitable hardware can participate in mining. The mining process involves compiling recent transactions into blocks and trying to solve a computationally difficult puzzle or algorithm. The participant who first solves the puzzle gets to place the next block on the block chain and claim the rewards. The rewards, which incentivize mining, are both the transaction fees associated with the transactions compiled in the block as well as newly released bitcoin. (Source: Investopedia.com).

Mining Algorithm – The algorithm used by a cryptocurrency to sign transactions, these vary across different cryptocurrencies. Bitcoin's mining algorithm is SHA256, whilst Litecoin & Dogecoin's are Scrypt.

Miner – A computer participating in any cryptocurrency network performing proof of work. This is usually done to receive block rewards.

Mining Pool – A group of miners who have decided to combine their computing power for mining. This allows rewards to be distributed more consistently between participants in the pool.

Mining Contract – A method of investing in bitcoin mining hardware, allowing anyone to rent out a pre-specified amount of hashing power, for an agreed amount of time. The mining service takes care of hardware maintenance, hosting and electricity costs, making it simpler for investors.

Minting – The process of rewarding users in proof of stake coins. New coins are minted as the reward for verifying transactions in a block.

Mixing Service – See "laundry"

Mobile Wallet – A wallet which runs a "mobile client", allowing people to have bitcoin wallets on their phones and tablet computers and pay on the go.

Money Laundering – The act of trying to "clean" money earned from criminal activity by converting these profits to what appear to be legitimate assets.

Mt. Gox – A bitcoin exchange based in Japan that collapsed in February 2014 due to poor security practices and incompetent management. Managed by Mark Karpeles.

Multisig – or multi-signature refers to having more than one signature to approve a transaction. This form of security is beneficial for a company receiving money into their BTC wallet. If a company wants to keep it so that one employee doesn't have sole access to a transaction, multi-set allows for a transaction to be verified by two separate employees before it's complete.

N

Namecoin – An altcoin which implemented a distributed DNS (domain name system) amongst other features. This distributed DNS helps people using the .bit domain to resist internet censorship. Can also be used to refer to the unit of currency NMC.

Network Effect – The increase in value of a good or service that occurs when its use becomes more widespread.

NFC – Acronym for "Near Field Communication", a low power, short range method of wireless communication. This can be used to build upon RFID systems and is what contactless smart cards (oyster cards) and payment systems (paypass) use. Most recently implemented in the Apple Pay app.

Node – A computer that connects to a cryptocurrency network and helps to verify the Blockchain's accuracy.

Nonce – A random number used once when a miner attempts to hash a transaction block. The parameters of these numbers are set by the "difficulty".

O

Off Blockchain Transactions – Exchanges of value which occur off the blockchain between trusted parties. These occur because they are quicker and do not bloat the blockchain.

Orphaned Block – A valid block which is discarded by the network after the blockchain has "forked" and then re-achieved consensus on a single blockchain again. This usually happens after two miners simultaneously solve a block, temporarily resulting in two valid blocks in the blockchain.

Open Source – The practice of sharing the source code for a piece of computer software, allowing it to be distributed and altered by anyone.

OTC exchange – Stands for "Over the Counter". These exchanges are places where trading is done directly between the two parties involved in the transaction, allowing traders to escape some of the limitations set by trading on formalized exchanges.

Output – The part of the transaction which contains instructions for the sending of bitcoin.

P

Paper wallet – A form of "cold storage" where the private keys are printed onto a piece of paper and stored offline.

Peercoin – The first cryptocurrency to implement "Proof Of Stake" alongside Proof Of Work.

P2P – Peer to Peer Network is another way of saying Peer-to-Peer. Peer-to-peer has become a very large focus of blockchain as one of the biggest selling points is decentralization. Nearly every interaction on the blockchain can be fulfilled P2P, or without a centralized variable like a store, bank or notary.

Pre-mining – The mining of a cryptocurrency by its developers before it is released to the public. This can be done with good intentions, however it is also strongly associated with scam coins.

Price Bubble – An economic cycle in which the price of a security or asset will surge unsustainably, and then crash as a selloff occurs. This is usually caused by speculation, and has been observable in bitcoin's past prices. When done deliberately, this is known as a "Pump and Dump"

Private Key – A secret series of letters and numbers kept by the owner of the crypto currency that allows it to be spent by the owner. This should be kept secret at all times.

Proof of Burn – This is a method of "burning" one Proof of Work cryptocurrency in order to receive a different cryptocurrency. This is a form of "bootstrapping" one cryptocurrency off another, and is done by sending coins to a verifiable unspendable address.

Proof of Existence – A service provided through the blockchain that allows anyone to anonymously and securely store a proof of existence for any document they choose online. This allows people to prove that a document existed at a certain point in time and demonstrate their ownership of it, without fear of that proof being taken from them.

Proof of Stake – An alternative to Proof of Work, providing an alternative method for deciding who signs transactions into the blockchain. In Proof of Stake, the resource held by the "miner" is their stake in the currency. So someone holding 10% of a proof of stake currency is equivalent to controlling 10% of the network hash rate of a Proof of Work currency.

Proof of Work – This is the type of mining algorithm Bitcoin uses, and is a method of determining who signs transactions in the blockchain. The Proof of Work scheme used by bitcoin is SHA256, a cryptographic hashing function.

Proof of Work, Proof of Stake – Proof of work and proof of stake are 2 algorithms for reaching consensus across a blockchain – To ensure the safety, security, incorruptibility and anonymity of cryptocurrencies being traded without the need for a centralized database or bank, there needs to be a way prove your work (PoW) or prove that you have a stake (PoS)

Public Key – A unique address consisting of numbers and letters that you give out to receive crypto currencies.

Pump and Dump – A form of market manipulation usually performed on small market cap stocks (or cryptocurrencies). This occurs when traders artificially inflate the assets price and then exit their positions, causing a price collapse.

Q

Quantitative easing – A form of monetary policy where a Central Bank purchases government securities with cash which did not exist before, in order to increase the money supply and lower interest rates.

QR code – Acronym for "Quick Response" code, these are 2d barcodes which can have data encoded onto them.

R

Remittance – A sum of money being sent, usually internationally, as a payment or gift.

Ripple – An alternative payment network to Bitcoin based on similar cryptography. The ripple network uses XRP as currency, and is capable of sending any asset type.

S

Satoshi – The smallest unit of a bitcoin currently available (0.00000001BTC).

Satoshi Nakamoto – The mysterious creator of Bitcoin. Known to possess over a million bitcoins, his/her/their/its identity is still unknown.

Scamcoin – Coins created as get rich quick schemes by their developers. These coins usually have certain properties, such as being clones of an existing coin and being pre-mined.

Scrypt – An alternative Proof of Work scheme to SHA256. This mining algorithm is used by Litecoin, Dogecoin and many other cryptocurrencies. Originally touted as being "ASIC resistant" due to its heavier memory requirements, ASICs have now been released for mining Scrypt.

Seed – The private key used in a "deterministic wallet"

Self executing contract – Also known as "smart contracts" these are protocols that facilitate or enforce the obligations of a contract without the need for human intervention.

Segwit (Segregated Witness) – an improvement to the core way

Bitcoin handles transactions in order to make the Bitcoin network approve more transactions with each block.

Sidechain – These are theoretical, independent blockchains which are "two way pegged" to the Bitcoin blockchain. These can have their own unique features and can have bitcoins sent to and from them.

Signature – Is the mathematical operation that lets someone prove their sole ownership over their wallet, coin, data or on. An example is how a Bitcoin wallet may have a public address, but only a private key can verify with the whole network that a signature matches and a transaction is valid. These are only known to the owner and are basically mathematically impossible to uncover.

Silk Road – The online marketplace where drugs and other illicit items could be traded for Bitcoin. Accessible through "TOR", Silk Road was shut down in October 2013 by the FBI.

Smart Contract – A two way smart contract is an unalterable agreement stored on the blockchain that has specific logic operations akin to a real world contract. Once signed, it can never be altered. A smart contract can be used to define certain computational benchmarks or barriers that have to be met in turn for money or data to be deposited or even be used to verify things such as land rights.

Speculator – An individual who speculates on the price of bitcoin or any other form of asset. Aiming to make profits by buying and selling at different prices.

SPV – Acronym for "Simplified Payment Verification", this allows mobile clients to make payments without needing a copy of the entire blockchain.

Stale Block – A block that has already been solved and thus cannot offer miners any reward for further work on it.

Soft Fork – A change to the operating protocol for a cryptocurrency that is backward compatible, so older nodes that don't upgrade will still function.

T

Taint – A measure of correlation between two addresses, this is used in attempts to track a coin's history.

TCP/IP – Acronyms stand for "Transmission Control Protocol"/"Internet Protocol" and is the connection protocol used by the internet.

Testnet – An alternative blockchain on which developers can test and experiment with changes to a cryptocurrency without the risk of damaging or interfering with the real blockchain.

Timestamp – A proof that a piece of data existed at a certain point in time. For Bitcoin this is the cryptographic proof of when transactions have taken place.

TOR – Stands for "The Onion Router" and is a free web browser designed to protect users anonymity and resist censorship. Allowing them to surf the web anonymously and access sites on the "deepweb".

Total Coin Supply – For many cryptocurrencies, there is a limit on the total number of coins that will ever come into existence, bitcoin's total supply is capped at 21 million coins.

Transaction Block – A group of transactions that are collected and hashed on the Bitcoin network by being added to the blockchain.

Transaction Fee – An amount of money users can choose to deduct from their transaction when sending money. This is optional and used to give miners incentive to quickly process their transaction, since they receive the fee as a reward for doing so.

V

Vanity Address – A bitcoin address which contains a desired word/ pattern or sequence of numbers. Kind of like a customized number plate.
Example: 1JAMES2K4rWaduCmCds36ox2VXdeBE7LNd

Velocity of Money – The velocity of money is an indicator of how quickly money received is then spent again. For bitcoin, we use "bitcoin days destroyed" to measure its velocity, this can indicate whether people are hoarding or spending their bitcoins.

Venture Capitalist – Can refer to an individual or organization that provide initial funding for start-up business ventures that cannot access public funding. This money is known as "seed funding", and is usually exchanged for equity in the start-up.

Virgin Bitcoin – A bitcoin that has been received by a miner as a block reward, and thus has never been "spent" before.

Volatility – A measure of fluctuations in price of a financial instrument over time. High volatility in bitcoin is seen as risky since its shifting value discourages people from spending or accepting it.

W

Wallet – A storage facility for cryptocurrencies. There are a number of different kinds of wallets; web wallets, desktop wallets, hardware wallets, mobile wallets, paper wallets and brain wallets.

Whitepaper – A report or guide made to understand an issue or help decision making. Satoshi Nakamoto released the whitepaper on

Bitcoin, titled "Bitcoin: A Peer-to-Peer Electronic Cash System" in late 2008.

Wire Transfer – An electronic method of transferring money from one party to another.

Z

Zerocoin – A project aimed at implementing true anonymity into the Bitcoin network.

Zero Confirmation transaction – A bitcoin transaction that has been relayed to nodes in the Bitcoin network but has not yet been incorporated into a block. Also known as "unconfirmed transactions".

NOTES

CPSIA information can be obtained
at www.ICGtesting.com
Printed in the USA
LVHW061514160519
618043LV00018B/159/P